HALLUCINATING

CARICATURES

(Leadership & Healthcare poems)

HALLUCINATING CARICATURES

(Leadership & Healthcare poems)

VICTOR EHIGHALEH

HALLUCINATING CARICATURES

Copyright © 2016 by Victor Ehighaleh. All rights reserved.

To leaders and everyone who has a medical challenge.

Contents

Foreword

"Hallucinating Caricatures" in a new poetic style, exposes the ills of our society. The author highlights the rat race among politicians to govern, even when they have zero knowledge of governance. Situations of healthcare delivery are also depicted.

Dispensaries abound but without drugs. Hospital patients are in agony without money to buy drugs, while medical professionals are in hot rivalry for leadership. The drunk and chain smokers in the poem is a sad reflection of a section of our society, who does not care for their health.

On the whole, the poems are written in a lucid language, easy to understand. It is recommended for all and sundry.

- John Olu Adeosun (JP)

Pregnant Life

Life gives life,

Noble objective to multiply,

Fruitfulness a command,

Good for all and sunder.

The beginning a mystery,

Gynecologists at arm's length,

Obstetricians waiting at the corner,

Mother basking in euphoria.

Emblem of pain for sale,

Sordid and pleasant,

Terrifying but an inviting game,

Life must go on.

Win at last a focus,

Driveway full of mines,

Detonation is time dependent,

Cat allays the fear of mouse.

Journey of hope indeed,

Mountain of valley awaiting mother,

Simultaneously crying and laughing,

Joy is beyond pain.

A fantasy sure and unveiled,

Deeper than a rig,

The ocean is too small for the ship,

Cut and mend to the rescue.

Cry, cry, but joy at last,

Impeccable freedom for the two,

Visitors lurking at the junction,

Tortoise smartness on the prowl.

The husband of some sort,

Millipede faster than a jet,

The eagle a master for the chick,

Walks as fast as a jet.

Eyes open but blind,

Two years down the line,

Another journey to labor,

Chain of pains continues.

Bullets downward from sky,

The torch is beaming darkness,

Darkness on front burner,

True luck available on discovery.

Face of lion beams smile,

A recipe for anarchy,

Killer road, hidden beneath the sky,

Ultimate food for the ants.

A smooth path to the frying pan,

Pains all the way,

Crooked as it unfolds,

Meal agape for the lions.

A single cry visible,

Attempts at resuscitation,

Journey of no return,

Baby in and out.

Mother awakens but frightened,

Living but appreciates death,

A vegetable of some sort,

The moon dries the clothes.

A fatherless pregnancy,

War invited to win,

Jeopardy let loose,

The black has turned to white.

Three legs mightier than ten,

A hydra stronger than iron,

The water solidifies,

Too cold for comfort.

Between the ice and water,

Which is superior?

The dwarf rule the giants,

A viral control of the genius.

An inviting car lacking engine,

Curtailing hot bullets using an umbrella,

A deep alley indeed,

Only a food for thought.

Woman must give birth,

Even after child's death,

The cycle continues,

Life is of necessity.

Sun and rain endlessly co-habiting,

A gang up too many,

An expressway to nowhere,

A delight for some.

Toga falls with glamour,

Better beneath than above,

Water sucking sugar,

The eyes are open.

She cries amusingly,

He is visible but mindless,

Vibrating words but empty,

Profits at making the snakes unhappy.

Sun moon and stars on the floor

Will not change the equation,

She must continue to give birth,

Nature abhors a vacuum.

Words entering paper,

Decree signed and sealed,

Cover unfolds and enclosed,

Finality on rampage.

Open and Mend

Come in different sizes and propensity,

Some minor others major,

A size lies in- between,

Success is the goal.

The ambience is morose,

Everyone is serious,

A few hallucinating and majority at alert,

Movement is endless.

Theater preparation ongoing,

Army already mobilized,

Innuendoes and after thought considered,

Life must go on.

Behind the screen is active,

Phone blaring and nodding,

Successful wish on the prowl,

Note of finality promising.

Progenitors let loose,

Time ticks away,

Zero hour beckons,

Waiting game commences.

Blood pressure let loose,

Who is the patient?

Anything can happen,

Patients on increase.

Gladiators professionally active,

Lights must not go out,

Failure is not an option,

Integrity is at stake.

The eyes of the wise is as deep as the ocean,

Joy and deceit as sweet as monkey pranks,

When discovered, becomes putrefying and sore,

Surgeons are able.

One in the pit is a lesson for others,

To be forewarned is to be forearmed,

Life waits for no one,

Surgeons on the prowl.

Operation successful at last,

Relatives embark on the return journey,

Journey outside oblivion,

Welcome home afresh.

Fear is bitter to behold,

Experience, an eye opener,

Too close to call,

Accomplishment a food for thought.

Victory party at last,

No longer the same,

Surgeons are great,

Nature opens afresh.

Care by Care

Who cares?

A discovery question,

Experience is an instructor,

Knowledge unlimited.

Independence at give away,

Others inhabit centre stage,

Merciless sea waves approach,

Destination unknown.

The caring needs care,

Compassion not common to behold,

Few possess the gold,

Amazing care givers.

Who needs care?

The loving needs care,

The caring needs love,

We all need to care.

Nurses are rare,

A collection of the called,

Living for others,

Light at end of tunnel.

The day begins with love,

Encounters like Amazon,

Discoveries by minute,

An endless show of love.

Journey to Known Unknown

Unveiling speed jet-like,

Serious looking and pain- propelled mortals,

Sea of concerned relatives unabated,

Moving but hurting.

Tragedy beckons,

No one to rescue,

Fatality let loose,

Time is of essence.

Ambulance more popular than a chicken tooth,

Lives languish in horror,

Known has become unknown,

The end beckons.

No plan implied,

Anger on discovery,

The guilty is shifting the blame,

An irony indeed.

Imbecile among imbeciles,

Familiarity breeds contempt,

Better than no one,

Equal among equals.

Unfolding world applauding,

History of no relevance,

What goes must go on,

House of commotion.

Kick the stones,

Complain not expected,

But the stones speak,

Drama in the world.

Dispensary

Health condition indicated,

The doctors have a say,

Nurses and laboratory scientists play their part,

No drugs, efforts in futility.

Dispensers in white apparel,

Looking smart and friendly,

Professionals to the core,

White must be white.

An impeccable background indeed,

Chemistry of drug interactions abound,

Drug and drug, food and drug,

Contra-indications all the way.

Restoration of health paramount,

Contribution to life is final,

Food on table,

Arising from contribution.

The dispenser, friend of manufacturers,

Marketers and dispenser is like three and four,

Marketers smile, meeting dispensers need,

A win-win of some sort.

The patient is crying to the banks,

The marketer smiling to the banks,

A cycle that must continue,

We are all involved.

Health is wealth,

Play your part,

Collective smiling possible,

Nature at play.

Aspiration

Human wants insatiable,

Everyone wants to lead,

A leader at a time,

No one wants to wait.

Endless show of force,

The order of the day,

Struggling to nowhere,

As sure as the air we breathe.

Nature, an ordered arrangement,

Learn from the ants,

Time waits for no one,

Utilize every opportunity.

The light flashes,

Only at long intervals,

The awake appreciates,

A game for the smart.

Cells too many to handle,

Shining but cancerous,

Pillar broom sticks beneath the iron,

A journey of death in focus.

Violence on peaceful slide,

Sea below, a broken pot,

A collection of vibrating emblem,

Too hot to handle.

Absolute risk ajar,

War looms,

Wait for your time,

One space at a time.

Teaching Hospital

The teaching hospital a theatre,

Hydra- headed characters abound,

Some pleasant and motivating,

Others a sorry sight to behold.

Yet, the tertiary, a peak,

Orchestra of the best,

Suction sustainer and initiator,

Attractiveness of some sort.

The future domiciles here,

Our tomorrow is harbored,

Building power house of future,

The layer of golden eggs.

A harbinger of complexities,

Difficult to understand,

Perpetual research ongoing,

When shall it end?

You are allowed to play your part,

Let the end determine itself,

Between the train and track,

Which comes first?

A question for tomorrow,

Just like the egg and chick,

Which comes first?

Eternity will produce the answer.

Between the doctors, nurses, pharmacists and others,

Who leads?

A volatile topic of our time,

Peace and progress all the way.

The patients, not interested in the vibrations,

A serene environment is of utmost necessity,

Restoration of health,

The only concern.

Be isolated from bickering promoters,

They fight parochially,

Our health must be restored,

Management has a duty.

The chief medical officer,

One head, different directions,

Uphill task maintaining sanity,

If not for tenure.

Tenure elongation, license for insomnia,

Nature comes to play,

Mother Nature of our dreams,

Escape route for problems.

Complex country within a country,

Programmed chaos effectively managed,

Chief medical officer,

An amazing job to do.

The meeting point of chains unbroken,

Iron beads that unify,

Only for synergy,

The rest, a story for another day.

Road junctions too numerous,

Misadventure, possible sometimes,

The wise blaze the trail,

Return to the conventional.

Protruding characters abound,

Some comic, some serious and others undecided,

Conforming apparels everywhere,

Some white, others blue among the group.

Qualifications to lead, not a tea party,

Proficiency in people and skills management is crucial,

A committee of brains,

Indeed let loose.

Different interests and characters,

Compulsorily under a canopy,

Compulsion, the deciding factor,

Everyone has a role.

Nurses, pharmacists and record staff meet,

Laboratory, laundry, sanitation, and security rally round,

Mortuary, information, research and transport collect the baton,

Eatery, porters, library and administration applaud.

The medics on training,

Another ball game,

The hope for the future,

Future begins with them.

Appearing innocent and vibrant,

Appropriate indoctrination ongoing,

Looking forward to enter the shoes,

Lay down by mentors.

The challenges are rigorous,

Everyday almost different,

Amazing kettle of fish,

Horizon to be endured.

Contending with academics,

Practical teachings, research and seminars,

Perpetually ongoing,

Freedom in sight.

About to continue the cycle,

Unending cycle indeed,

Human wants insatiable,

Perpetuity on riot.

Diagnostic powerhouse at other end,

Radiology department critical,

Abounding in enclosure,

Yet powerful and germane.

Chemical pathology and biochemistry,

Microbiology, the infinity lookers,

Swimming with samples suspiciously,

Careful to avoid contamination and infection.

A house full of chains,

Chains so dependent and important,

The synergy is potent,

It must not be broken.

Be Determined

To the gullible,

Waking up is as sure as sunset,

The horizon must appear,

Failure is not an option.

To the wise,

Waking up is not a right,

It is like an election between two candidates,

Anything can happen.

The world is pregnant with surprises,

Preparation is positive,

Wisdom is of critical essence,

As you make your bed, so you lie on it.

Plant your seeds on time,

Await appropriate harvest,

He who sows apple cannot reap wheat,

Nature is just.

The beginning is important,

Tail end, determined by mid life,

Finishing well an option,

Nature is just.

Journey began with outcome in view,

Pros and cons on the table,

Wandering about checkmated,

Wisdom does not come cheap.

Pay the requisite price,

Be enthusiastic as a chick surrounded by grains,

The one with strong legs is not lame,

Success is sure.

The Drunk

He wakes up propelled by yesterday,

His wisdom amazingly deficient,

Every other person is a fool,

He is the problem.

Terminal illness beckons,

Eyes open but full of illusions,

Moments of pleasure, more important,

Days of reckoning surreptitiously waiting.

The day begins on a bright but clumsy note,

Other mortals are increasingly strange,

He pushes over ultimate medical condition,

The present must be enjoyed.

Silent hypertension and diabetes brewing,

Daily physical and emotional pleasures continues,

Completely oblivious of reality,

Absolutely submerged in a dream world.

Wakes up more drowsy than ever,

Dentition requires attention,

As sure as food for the belly,

He makes a momentary but expected slump.

The infirmary awaits a visitor,

A visit without return,

Product of needless indulgence,

Nature is just.

Smoke

Grew up in a smoke environment,

Smoke, like oxygen for existence,

A day without smoke, not realistic,

Everywhere is smoke.

Nicotine addiction, a way of life,

Solitary confinement in a world of smoke,

Food is of lesser importance,

Smoke all the way.

A day without smoke,

Like a dog giving birth to an elephant,

Absent life in a better world,

Tragedy personified.

Those who stray to smoke,

Share the pregnant tragedy,

Be mindful of your visits,

Consequences too grave to jettison.

Cancer of the lungs,

As friendly as cat and mouse,

Do you love it?

The pit is open! Make a choice!

The world must awake,

Enough of needless deaths,

You are very important,

A word is enough for the wise.

Protruding Mien

The joy of today, the pain of tomorrow,

It comes seamlessly and unnoticed,

In various sizes and hiccup shapes,

Vanity unlimited.

The ego stands akimbo,

Sucking moth on rampage,

Before the daybreak,

Intravenous damage, colossal and incredible.

At conception, an embodiment of excellence,

Like the early morning sun, a tonic for the bones,

Intransigent habits, redirect the traction,

A protruding belly without life is an empty shell.

No use for protrusion, giving birth to morbid,

Production of concomitantly unfolding anomalies,

More calories required to keep load afloat,

Wasted energy indeed.

The free should stay free,

Avoid journey to known crisis,

Only the blind will proceed,

A word is enough for the wise.

Change

Behind the curtains,

Dominant powers blossom,

The republic appears endless,

All conquered, increasingly decimated.

The pseudo silent group awakens,

Planning rebellion underneath,

The crescent is noticeable,

Only to discerning minds.

The agitated, on the increase,

Unfolding scenario is dangerous,

Who can stem the tide?

Time is pregnant.

Gathered storms are unveiling,

Too clear to avoid,

Too smart to miss,

The truth is obvious.

The game changer comes alive,

Amalgamation of old and new,

A hybrid of a sort,

Accepted by the majority.

Third level rebellion emanates,

Plot against pseudo leaders,

The betrayers are betrayed,

The smart at their game.

Burning issues highlighted,

Only by privileged few,

The majority at crossroad,

New leaders on the prowl.

Consciousness becomes electrifying,

Followers all over terrain,

Rolling stone gathering momentum,

Outcome as clear as light.

Those who want to lead,

Must be schooled to lead,

Between the egg and chick,

Which comes first?

The hand of clock is ticking,

No going back,

Forward ever,

Backward never.

The Republic

The inspiration is nonetheless awesome,

Everything is absolutely in place,

The pregnant are delivered,

The lame are walking.

Pleasant surprises, daily occurrence,

Leaders ravishing in glory,

Endlessly celebrated,

Legends, truly expressed.

Lack of experience suddenly manifests,

Managing success requires maturity,

The chickens are too young to act,

The deep appears unavoidable.

The journey down slope unfolds,

The young believe they are able,

They cruise on the wide and narrow path,

Catastrophe is slowly on arrival.

The elders are not consulted,

The cabal knows it all,

The endpoint is certain,

Beneath the deep blue sea.

Calculated drowning commence slowly,

Colleagues noticed danger,

The greedy, having a rendezvous,

Absolutely unconscious of the obvious.

A great and promising entity journeys under,

The elders, promptly caution,

Those with ears acted otherwise,

Reality is hunting.

Management seeks for help,

Help increasingly belated,

The hole in teeth; too deep to fill,

Uproot, the only option.

Apparent pains of uproot, terrible,

The thought of it is electrocution prone,

Yet, no escape,

Pain you must have.

Days of rhapsody are gone,

The deaf ears have become obsolete,

Suddenly, they want to cooperate,

Sorry, it is too late.

Foolishness visits,

Intimate friends, play betrayal game,

The centre in disarray,

Wisdom is not cheap.

The outstanding advice at inception,

Thrown out mockingly and vindictively,

The early wise have become foolish,

A funny world indeed.

Wisdom does not come cheap,

Pay the price,

Easy way often ends in gravel in mouth,

A word is enough for the wise.

No one is an island,

Together, we are better,

Put on your thinking cap,

Consultation is a key.

The ants are good at it,

Learn from them,

Wisdom is not cheap,

Wake up from slumber.

The good in us is crying for release,

Give it the deserved attention,

Failure is an orphan,

A word is enough for the wise.

Move along the right path,

Like a rolling stone, gathering momentum,

Affecting lives positively,

Sustain the tempo.

Produce enduring fruits,

Fruits for propagation,

Collectively, let's move on,

We are better together.

Rays

Multicolored and glittering lighted paths,

Darkness gone to the unknown forest,

The days of boom are born forever,

The ambience presents a sea smile.

New country goes berserk,

In need of cosmopolitan inhabitants,

Friendly mortals, seamlessly required,

The gap is crying for habitation.

New frontiers opened at last,

Intending pilgrims petrified and confused,

Horizon clamoring for relevance,

Like the post war era.

The unknown is far but tempting,

Present travails cumbersome,

The known is stale,

Movements ooze out of the stale.

Tempting sky is milky blue,

Topography undulating across the ocean,

Sight of shadows almost endless,

The future is pregnant and unknown.

Little hands outstretched and waving,

Welcome to the new world!

The habitation of prosperity,

Silent quakes are hidden beneath.

Top creamy and inviting,

Middle, deeper than a rig,

Danger inhabits the third layer,

Snares are everywhere.

Ruler

The flowers are falling apart,

Outside the time,

Who is responsible?

The snail about to sail.

Governance is left for mediocre,

The qualified, on holidays,

Hallucinations all the way,

Who will deliver the snail?

The fish sights the hook,

It appears rewarding,

A free party,

Waterloo is looming.

Mouth agape, death approaching,

Hey, eat and die,

Not all that glitters is gold,

Beware of free food.

A leader requires wisdom,

Empty shells not needed,

Not a tea party,

It is knowledge driven.

The choice is open to all,

You have a right to vote and be voted for,

Not negotiable,

Use it wisely.

Hallucinating Caricatures

The game end is unknown,

Wakes up fearfully agitated,

The work of yesterday resonates,

Reality awakens the mortal.

The journey is pregnant with doubts,

Eyes are opened but disillusioned,

Seeing stars but cannot comprehend,

The journey is comprehensive.

The small animals, a bit noisy,

Animal kingdom unfolding,

The journey must continue,

The unknown, available to pursue.

The situation is frightening,

The creature in him must arise,

Time is of essence to the living,

The end must be resolutely determined.

The secret of yesterday is known to him,

Yet the fears of tomorrow overwhelming,

Like the journey to the lion's den,

The reward is good, only for the victor.

If you must conquer, do not fidget,

The determined and focused, good to go,

Though obstacles present themselves,

Victory is like waking from sleep.

The owner of your waking,

Understands your tomorrow,

The events and innuendoes are clear to him,

Arise and set out.

The one who enjoyed a forty dollars meal,

Is now uncomfortable,

Visits the convenience,

Reality oozing out.

Trepidation, a companion,

The present is clear and continuous,

The journey begins to unfold,

The infirmary awaits a guest.

The ones he love are informed,

A confused atmosphere overwhelms,

Time increased the trepidation,

Reality - infirmary let loose.

He looks at past scenes,

His mistakes unfold only to him,

He gnashes his browning dentition,

The noise of a crack apparent.

He beckons to his bone of bone,

She laments,

Emotions let loose,

Maturity in want of evidence.

Picture becomes clear to all,

Infirmary journey is instant,

Clear agreement, appears without word,

The house, move on.

Car keys find relevance,

Extremely useful at the moment,

Required to rescue the household,

The head is in disarray.

Journey to the unknown commences,

Acoustic noise overwhelms,

The unfolding scenery, is dark,

The infirmary is waiting.

The road ahead is clearly determined,

The chauffeur cruise at top speed,

Pains escalate,

Bone of bone emoting.

Upcoming patient, disillusioned,

Palpable fear is invited,

The reality is as clear as ever,

Infirmary awaits the family.

Cruise to a lighted highway,

Green life disintegrating,

It comes to an abrupt end,

Surprise is the chauffeur's lot.

Patient hallucinating,

Sounds of the impact is confusing,

Childhood days resonate,

Beats are provoking.

Wish to end the trip,

Only a wish in futility,

Journey is appropriate,

The discerning mind is sure.

Car beckons on all,

The red is reality,

Read light on dashboard,

A gas station is required.

Short distance ahead,

Fuel lid, goes ajar,

Gas happily transits,

Belly regurgitate expectedly.

Journey afresh,

Interruption necessary,

Hallucinations continue,

Wish the saga ends.

Sights policemen ahead,

Three blue clothed men,

Chauffeur slows down,

Interrogation is sure.

The sick, is a sorry sight,

The blue men agree,

Interruption is over,

Back on track.

Bone of bone increasingly emoting,

Wish it was a dream,

Unfortunately not,

Mercy takes flight.

Patient is silent awhile,

Bone of bone hallucinating,

Chauffeur not perturbed,

Has a job at hand.

He intuitively increased mileage,

Patient makes come back,

Wife feels better,

Pleasant hiccups.

A changed atmosphere,

Good to behold,

Pain postponed but appears in ten seconds

Back to square one.

Journey appears unending,

Fifteen minutes appear fifty,

The confusion escalates,

Infirmary gate sighted afar.

Bone of bone feels better,

The sight ahead is a bit far,

The pleasantries good for the moment,

Ultimate journey commencing.

Infirmary gate personnel is alive,

Promptly and professionally agitated,

Amazingly alive,

Car exits them.

Route opens,

Chauffeur press right buttons,

Car jerks to a stop,

Arms waiting.

Protocols explode,

Record personnel comes alive,

Documentation completes,

Ultimate approval.

The doctor on call is notified,

Hormones about to explode,

Adrenaline implied,

Oh! A high school classmate.

A job at hand,

Competence ooze out,

Emotions take flight,

Forward is good to go.

Preliminary investigations ongoing,

Bone of bone responsive,

Infirmary ambience adaptable,

Sigh of relief walks in.

First line investigations released,

Too bad, emotions rise again,

Professionalism to the rescue,

Going forward is the only option.

Further tests are required,

Referrals for confirmation,

Samples prepare to develop legs,

To embark on the journey.

Urine, collected and part of skin sterilized,

Gentle pricking of flesh occurs,

Escape of blood,

Red sample separated from reservoir.

Stool, also wanted,

The patient agitated,

Cooperation required,

Reluctantly complies.

Pink, red and yellow samples walking,

Knocks at laboratory doors,

Chemical pathology and microbiology,

Simultaneously, door ajar.

Eagle eyes at work,

Results emanate,

Too bad for comfort,

A bombshell indeed.

Results run to doctor,

She peruses with anxiety,

Oh! More tests,

The unknown is becoming real.

Ultrasound scan of kidney indicated,

Potters erupt in anxiety,

Patient moved to site,

Radiology awaits a guest.

Professionals at work,

Equipments engaged,

Staff vibrant and enthusiastic,

Work in progress.

Team leader surprised,

Patient, a sixth grade classmate,

Childhood emotions implicated,

She has a job to do.

Emotions take flight,

The needful is accomplished,

Views kidney on computer,

Too bad for comfort.

Renal transplant is a friend,

She ruminates for a moment,

Kidney transplant!

Hope not lost.

Oh! Chronic kidney disease why?

ESRD – End stage renal disease,

Organ transplant let loose,

An amazing friend is waiting for survival.

Results presented to doctor on duty,

Peruse the findings,

Emotions alive again,

She remembers; professionalism on call.

Reality dawns on her,

Going forward is very necessary,

The options are very clear,

Kidney transplant.

Bone of bone is notified,

Hunts for donor,

She beckons on chauffeur,

Let us journey home.

Promptly excuse husband,

Consultations at arm's length,

Truth - out at last,

Action all the way.

Machineries set in motion,

Who will donate?

Family members consulted,

Who among the living is ready to donate?

The journey erupts,

A sibling to the rescue

Necessary samples on investigation,

Donor is compatible.

Journey to kidney harvest is fast forwarded,

Amazing sibling indeed,

Recipient awaits a foreigner,

He must accept by force.

Prior to this,

Doctor highlights specifics,

Medical jargons endlessly jumps out,

Bone of bone nods in confusion.

Patient will reject the transplant,

Immunosuppressive therapy to the rescue,

Immunity must be suppressed,

Counter rejection strategy.

Applaud for medical research,

Anti-rejection medications are available,

There is a price to pay,

Befriend the banks.

Throughout life of transplanted kidney,

Anti-rejection medications a life companion,

Away with them to your peril,

Staying alive is not a joke.

Immunosuppressive therapy has foes,

Eyes can see great infection risks,

Man on black apparel, presents a mallet,

Cancer and lymphoma.

Jargons almost endless,

For discerning minds alive,

Health is indeed wealth,

A word for the wise.

Bone of bone lesson ends,

Reality takes centre stage,

Donor must be prepared,

The recipient alike.

Screening successfully concluded,

Green lights appear,

Good to go!

Absolute subscription at play.

Kidney, already harvested,

Cardinal purpose comes alive,

Transplant surgery – three to five hours,

Three to five days for test run.

Between four and ten days is additional hospital stay,

Planning, a regiment,

At blast of whistle,

Anything can happen.

Recipient's wife ruminates on causes,

Diabetes mellitus, malignant hypertension,

Focal segmental glomerulosclerosis,

Endless jargons indeed.

Back to reality, fidgets over the success rate,

Thoughts of widowhood is strong,

She rejects it,

Husband is already in the theatre.

Transplant surgery kick- starts,

Every second appears endless,

Blood pressure on the rise,

She imagined her veins burst open.

Palpable fear smells,

She asks, what is happening?

Why am I going through this?

Theatre door opens.

Her heart, literally jump to her mouth,

Apprehension all over,

She rushed to the door,

Denied entry.

Traumatic surgery over at last,

Success light radiantly flashing,

Doctors, half accomplished,

Post – operative complications, the other half.

Next few days, on assessment,

Bleeding, infection, thrombosis among others,

Urinary abnormalities also critical,

Absolute jargons on the rise.

Finally, the coast is clear,

Surgery, effectively managed,

Another life is born,

Survival is for the masters.

Bone of bone is excited,

Back from the land of the dead,

She requested for water,

Joy at last.

She ruminates again,

I warned him about unhealthy eating habits,

It fell on deaf ears,

Almost made me a widow,

Obviously a needless journey,

If only he had listened to me,

Yet, she is relieved, if not for money,

Probably a different story.

Money developing hands,

Receivers are providing service,

A new life is born,

A win for the jugular.

www.ingramcontent.com/pod-product-compliance
Lightning Source LLC
Chambersburg PA
CBHW020747160726
47993CB00006B/2656